YOUR KNOWLEDGE HAS VALUE

Nicholas Williams

The Portrayal of William Rufus in the "Vita Anselmi" and Huntingdon's "Historia Anglorum"

GRIN Verlag

Bibliografische Information der Deutschen Nationalbibliothek:

Die Deutsche Bibliothek verzeichnet diese Publikation in der Deutschen National-
bibliografie; detaillierte bibliografische Daten sind im Internet über http://dnb.d-
nb.de/ abrufbar.

Imprint:

Copyright © 2006 GRIN Verlag GmbH
Druck und Bindung: Books on Demand GmbH, Norderstedt Germany
ISBN: 978-3-640-33889-4

This book at GRIN:

http://www.grin.com/en/e-book/127228/the-portrayal-of-william-rufus-in-the-vita-
anselmi-and-huntingdon-s-historia

GRIN - Your knowledge has value

Der GRIN Verlag publiziert seit 1998 wissenschaftliche Arbeiten von Studenten, Hochschullehrern und anderen Akademikern als eBook und gedrucktes Buch. Die Verlagswebsite www.grin.com ist die ideale Plattform zur Veröffentlichung von Hausarbeiten, Abschlussarbeiten, wissenschaftlichen Aufsätzen, Dissertationen und Fachbüchern.

Visit us on the internet:

http://www.grin.com/

http://www.facebook.com/grincom

http://www.twitter.com/grin_com

Special Subject Group:
Politics and Political Culture
in Norman and Angevin England
Essay no 2

The Portrayal of William Rufus in the *Vita Anselmi* and Huntingdon's *Historia Anglorum*

Williams Rufus, the second Norman king in England, did not strike a chord with his contemporary chroniclers and writers of history. Instead, he was portrayed as just about everything a monarch should not be. This changed in later centuries, but once his image had been set by eleventh and twelfth century writers, many others just drew on them, manifesting the negative picture that existed of William Rufus and reinterpreting it only in nuances.[1]

It is not the subject of this essay to retrace and follow this picture throughout the ages, although the conclusion will come back to this point. Instead, the focus here will be on two medieval writers who wrote about William Rufus, Eadmer and Henry of Huntingdon. A short passage will deal with their backgrounds and the key features of their work, so far as they are relevant to their attitudes towards William Rufus. The main body will look at passages written about William Rufus, taking into account the rhetoric and language involved, comparing where they differ and where they have similarities. The focus here will be a critical one, highlighting contradictions within and between the texts. Finally, the conclusion will again question both Eadmer's and Huntingdon's motives, and try evaluate the use of their accounts of Williams Rufus.

Both Henry of Huntingdon and Eadmer were writing from within the ecclesiastical community, but with different backgrounds and mindsets, as will be seen throughout this essay. This does not mean to say, however, that they were entirely different. Henry was married and in a way part of the "secular clergy," writing about things he himself read about, while Eadmer was a monk and very close to the "object" of his writing.[2]

It is hardly surprising that Eadmer did not take kindly to William Rufus, given the constant trouble between the king and the very man Eadmer was portraying as an immaculate saint. The first time he mentions William, it is with the words, "William oppressed the churches and monasteries throughout England most harshly."[3] On the following page, Eadmer describes the respect paid and tribute done to Anselm by William: "he [William] fell on his neck and led him by the hand to his seat."[4] According to Eadmer's account, Anselm then openly criticized the king for his treatment of the church and his homosexuality (sic!)[5], which the king tolerated and accepted.

---

[1] T. Callahan, The Making of a monster: the historical image of William Rufus, in: JMH 7 (1981), 175.
[2] This merely refers to Eadmer's *Vita Anselmi*, which is part of the subject of this essay, not his other historical writings.
[3] *Vita Amselmi*, 63.
[4] *Vita Anselmi*, 64.
[5] Ibid., 64.

Having thus taken certain liberties which others might (or might not!) have lived to regret, it follows neither from Eadmer's nor from Henry of Huntingdon's account why the "hated king,"[6] who "ended his cruel life with a wretched death"[7] and was "at the instigation of the devil and of evil men,"[8] little later declared that for the vacant archbishopric of Canterbury "Anselm was the man most fitted for this work."[9] One explanation could be that William was so ill that his death seemed more than likely, so that he was in fear of his soul. In this case, appointing Anselm, whose reputation as a saint was already in the making, as archbishop would seem a wise move.[10]

Henry of Huntingdon's first mention of William is, on the other hand, by far more favourable than Eadmer's:

> "William, going to Winchester, divided his father's treasure as he wished. In the treasury there was £ 60,000 in silver, in addition to gold, jewels, vessels, and hangings. Of this he gave to certain churches ten marks of gold, to others six, and to the church of each village 5s, and he sent to each county £ 100 to be distributed among the poor. He also freed all those bound in chains on his father's orders."[11]

However, such moves were later taken back, at least as far as the prisoners were concerned:

> "Any prisoners who had not yet been released he ordered to be guarded more strictly than ever, those already released, if they could be caught, were to be thrown again in prison (...) and tried by judges whose concern was more to subvert justice than to guard or defend it (...)"[12]

After the first struggle over power with William's brother Robert, whose allies Henry of Huntingdon condemns,[13] William Rufus took to political patterns reminiscent of those his father employed, namely the redistribution of his opponents' land to his own followers and supporters.[14] Moreover, Henry mentions that "the king assembled the English people, and restored to them the rights of hunting and forests, and promised them desirable laws."[15]

Initially, Henry of Huntingdon bore no grudge against William Rufus, on the contrary, on the first two pages of his account of the reign of William the younger, he presents him in neutral terms. Eadmer, in turn, would not have been writing the biography of an archbishop if William had not given his consent to Anselm's

---

[6] *Historia Anglorum*, 49.
[7] Ibid., *48*.
[8] *Vita Anselmi*, 67.
[9] Ibid., 64.
[10] R. Huscroft, Ruling England 1042-1217, Harlow et al. 2005, 65.
[11] *Historia Anglorum*, 33.
[12] Quoted from T. Callahan, The Making of a Monster, 176.
[13] Ibid., 35.
[14] Ibid., 36.
[15] Ibid., 35.

ordainment in the first place. Admittedly, the circumstances of Anselm's appointment were not quite the usual ones, and it may be left open to guess whether his famous reluctance to accept the office[16] was because he was wise enough to suspect there would be conflict.[17] Additionally, Eadmer was loyal to and a friend of Anselm for much longer than he was an archbishop.[18] However, it is worth asking what made Anselm fall out with the king and in which ways the two chroniclers' account of the conflict differ, and where their texts and views match.

Eadmer informs us that Anselm lost the king's favour because "he refused to despoil his tenants in order to give the king £ 1,000 as a thank-offering for his munificence."[19] The payment of such a sum would have deemed Anselm's takeover an act of simony, which was not uncommon (as long as a better name was found for it) but hardly acceptable for a man who even Henry of Huntingdon, who otherwise hardly mentions Anselm, called "a saintly and venerable man."[20] An interesting light on this debate is shed by Emma Mason, who generally speaks in William's defence against other historical judgement. She maintains that the sum demanded by William was a just request. Anselm's later refusal to pay the king money for his Welsh campaign she sees as contradicting his desire for jurisdiction over the Welsh clergy.[21] Naturally, there is no mention of such a desire by Eadmer.

The payment episode did obviously not go down well with the king. On their next meeting, Anselm sought William's help to relieve the churches – of what he remains vague.[22] It may therefore be assumed that Anselm voiced the wish for general support and reestablishment of a good relationship between king and church. Such a wish was not granted, and it seems that, as far as William was concerned, he already regarded his being ad odds with Anselm as a long-term state of affairs.

Henry of Huntingdon does not mention this initial row between Anselm and the king. However, he does record another act of simony concerning the bishopric of Lincoln, which he had given to Robert Bloet in 1093, the same year that Anselm had become archbishop. Having unexpectedly recovered from his illness, William at hindsight regretted he had given away this see with out demanding money too, so he

---

[16] *Vita Anselmi*, 64+65, R. Hushcroft, Ruling England, 65.
[17] Eadmer writes of "the many obstacles which stood in the way." (p. 66), suggesting multiple reasons for Anselm's hesitation to accept the archbishopric.
[18] R.W. Southern, Saint Anselm and his biographer. A Study of monastic life and thought 1059-c. 1130, Cambridge 1963, 229.
[19] *Vita Anselmi*, 67.
[20] *Historia Anglorum*, 37.
[21] E. Mason, William Rufus: myth and reality, in: JMH 3 (1977), 7.
[22] *Vita Anselmi*, 69.

sided with the archbishop of York when he claimed authority over Lincoln and Lindsey. This way, he extorted £ 5,000 from Robert Bloet "for the liberty of his church."[23] Henry of Huntingdon saw all the blame on the king's side, but as Henry's family was quite close to the same Robert Bloet, and given that the *Historia Anglorum* was commissioned by Bloet's successor, it is neither surprising that Henry mentioned this event (which occurred right on his doorstep) rather than the Anselm episode, nor that he saw all the blame on the king's side. Henry called the affair "an act of simony",[24] and it takes little imagination where Bloet found the money for the payment: within his archbishopric. Additionally, by paying, Robert was part of the deal, and Henry's claim that "the bishop behaved correctly"[25] is unlikely to have found overall consensus. It should also be noted that the accusation of simony was at the time both a political weapon and means of discredit, and that simony was as much on the agenda of the Gregorian Reform as was clerical marriage.[26] Henry was a married cleric, so his accusation against William Rufus looks, at least today, somewhat hypocritical.

It is not the purpose of this work to morally condemn medieval chroniclers. Instead, Henry's hypocrisy and Anselm's only telling one side of the story display something else: Their versions of William Rufus were instrumental to the broader pictures they intended to convey. Henry's declared view of Norman rule was that it was a punishment sent by God,[27] and history in general was in his view suitable to promote moral ends.[28] In other words, William Rufus needed to fit into this general picture, and where necessary, Henry made him fit, especially as William as a character was interpreted by him as the punishment the Normans themselves deserved in turn[29].

Eadmer, on the other hand, was writing the biography of a saint in whose service he was. He makes use of many literary figures and biblical rhetoric, ascribing to Anselm characteristic features usually attached to Jesus,[30] using Jesus' metaphors[31] and working miracles similar to those of Jesus.[32] In short: William could not win.

---

[23] *Historia Anglorum*, 37.
[24] Ibid., 37.
[25] Ibid., 37.
[26] LMA (=Lexikon des Mittelalters), CD-Rom edition, Stuttgart 2000, LexMA 7, 1923-1924.
[27] *Historia Anglorum*, 35.
[28] Ibid., Prologue, 1.
[29] *Historia Anglorum*, 35.
[30] *Vita Anselmi*, 15.
[31] Ibid., 16-20 + 57.
[32] Ibid., 23.

Praising Anselm to a description befitting a saint, Eadmer, in literary terms, needed a counterpart, a background against which the object of his praise would shine ever more brightly. Consequently, Anselm "burst into bitter tears"[33] on hearing that the king, effectively an enemy he had every reason to hate, had died. Additionally, Eadmer had good cause for making William's successor, Henry I, appear in a more favourable light, hence he ascribed Henry's motive for reconciliation with Anselm as the former being "moved both by fear and the love of God."[34] Anselm needed to reach some form of compromise with Henry,[35] therefore he had to fulfil minimum criteria to be worthy of negotiation at all. Again, a contrast was therefore necessary.

From the initial dispute on things between William and Anselm went from bad to worse. Initially, William had no intention to recognize Urban II as pope, while Anselm, at the council of Rockingham in 1095, publicly declared his support for him.[36] From Urban Anselm needed the archiepiscopal pallium in order to have full authority as archbishop. Anselm sought William's permission to go to Rome to receive it, and was unsurprisingly turned down: the archbishop, who was by no way in William's good books, was requesting permission to go and establish his authority from a pope the king did not recognize. Surprisingly, the king gave way. He finally recognized Urban II as pope and through intermediaries had the pallium delivered to Anselm.[37] This was about as much as Anselm could expect, and it was, as R.W. Southern points out, "Anselm's only political victory in Rufus's reign."[38] It was also a major humiliation of the king, who was bound not to forget, while Eadmer regarded it more as a tactical move.[39]

Anselm was still not satisfied and remained bent on going to Rome. He saw his relationship with the king permanently damaged and sought the pope's advice and help in protecting the church. The king refused, " 'for', he said, 'we have not found him so lacking in counsel in what needs to be done, that he must needs consult the pope, nor subject to any grave sin, for which he must implore his absolution.' "[40] Unsatisfied with the answer, Anselm renewed his request every time he met the king.

---

[33] Ibid., 126.
[34] Ibid., 134.
[35] R.W. Southern, Anselm and his biographer, 180.
[36] Vita Anselmi, 85.
[37] Ibid., 87.
[38] R.W. Southern, St Anselm and his biographer, 155.
[39] Vita Anselmi, 87.
[40] Ibid., 89.

This strategy was at best unimaginative, and the king thought it excessively tiring.[41] Finally, he gave in to Anselm's wearisome approach and let him go, on the understanding that in so doing Anselm was exiling himself.[42] After one final "baggage check" at his departure, ordered by the king,[43] Anselm left the country and the two never met again.

Henry of Huntingdon briefly mentions the episode in his *Historia Anglorum*, "then Archbishop Anselm left the country because the evil king would permit nothing right to be done in his kingdom."[44] Eadmer's and Henry of Huntingdon's accounts hardly overlap for the following years, as Henry then goes into a detailed description of the first crusade, while Eadmer recounts Anselm's years in exile in Rome and Lyon, where he achieved preciously little.[45] Whatever Henry of Huntingdon says about William Rufus, though, is not quite as negative as Eadmer's views. Henry writes about his numerous battles in a similar tone as he does about King Stephen.[46] He calls him "the energetic king"[47] on one occasion, a title he uses for King Stephen regularly.[48] Henry does not paint William as black as Eadmer does, but he does make it quite obvious he generally thinks little of his reign. However, he is more reasoned than Eadmer, and where he sees good done by the king, he does state so. Replying to a sailor who warned him of a dangerous channel crossing to come to the aid of the besieged La Mans, Henry has William say, " 'I have never heard tell of a king who drowned in the waves.' Then he crossed the sea and did nothing in his lifetime that brought him so much fame and glorious honour."[49] Obviously and despite his bias, Henry is more prepared than Eadmer to weigh good against bad, even though his conclusion is that William was a bad king.

It has been outlined in this essay that Eadmer and Henry came to different but similar judgments of William II. Emma Mason's accusation against William's contemporary chroniclers that the clergy effectively had the monopoly of writing history in the 12th century and that therefore all views of William should be revised[50] is hardly convincing. For these chroniclers, royal protection of the church was a key

---

[41] R.W. Southern, St Anselm and his biographer, 160.
[42] *Vita Anselmi*, 92.
[43] Ibid., 98.
[44] *Historia Anglorum*, 47.
[45] R.W. Southern, St Anselm and his biographer, 161.
[46] *Historia Anglorum, 36,38,47,48.*
[47] Ibid., 38.
[48] Ibid., 69, 78.
[49] Ibid., 48.
[50] E. Mason, William Rufus, 1.

issue, and the church as such was something not to be tampered with. Today, political systems are very much measured for their compliance with human rights. The values have changed, the bias has not. Therefore, Mason's conclusion that William Rufus was an effective politician is technically interesting, in terms of his value as a king however, we may still rely on ecclesiastical sources, as they measure him against 12th century criteria of what is good, and not those Machiavelli would have used.

Reading both Huntingdon and Eadmer critically still yields facts about William Rufus. After all, both mention events that would make him appear in a more favourable light: even through Eadmer's account it becomes clear that the king was not entirely uncompromising (or he would not have recognized Urban II as pope in the first place), and through the *Historia Anglorum* it becomes apparent that William did not waste his energies in the same way as Stephen of Blois did. This does not mean that, put together, they give a round and historically sound picture of William; however, reading one along with the other is sufficient to see that William was not a monster, and that Anselm had lost touch with the world too much to be an effective archbishop, an office which required political skill and realism, both hardly to be expected in a saint. William and Anselm barely understood one another at all and kept talking at cross purposes.[51] This is what becomes apparent from the *Vita Anselmi*. William was a ruthless but clever organiser; he had his faults but was by far better at maintaining royal authority than King Stephen was, this we can see from Henry of Huntingdon's *Historia Anglorum*.

---

[51] R.W. Southern, Anselm and his biographer, 155.

Bibliography

Primary Sources

- Henry of Huntingdon: The History of the English People 1000-1154, ed. and transl. by Diana Greenway, Oxford 2002.
- Eadmer: The Life of St Anselm, Archbishop of Canterbury, ed. and transl. by R.W. Southern, Oxford [2]1972.

Secondary Sources

- Callahan, Thomas: The Making of a monster: the historical image of William Rufus, in: JMH (= Journal of Medieval History) 7 (1981), 175-185.
- Huscroft, Richard: Ruling England 1042-1217, Harlow et al. 2005
- LMA (=Lexikon des Mittelalters), CD-Rom edition, Stuttgart 2000.
- Mason, Emma: William Rufus: myth and reality, in: JMH 3 (1977), 1-19.
- Southern, Richard William: Saint Anselm and his biographer. A Study of monastic life and thought 1059-c. 1130, Cambridge 1963.